THROUGHOUT *These Forty Days* WE PRAY

JOHN F. O'GRADY

Paulist Press
New York/Mahwah, NJ

Cover and book design by Lynn Else

Library of Congress Cataloging-in-Publication Data

O'Grady, John F.
 Throughout these forty days we pray / John F. O'Grady.
  p. cm.
 ISBN-13: 978-0-8091-4510-2 (alk. paper)
 1. Lent—Prayers and devotions. 2. Lent—Meditations. 3. Common lectionary (1992) I. Title.
 BV85.O37 2008
 242'.34—dc22

                                                                2007020809

Published by Paulist Press
997 Macarthur Boulevard
Mahwah, New Jersey 07430

www.paulistpress.com

Printed and bound in the
United States of America

Contents

Contents

Dedication

*To Sister Noreen Mangan, IHM, and the
O'Gradys she taught:*

J. Patrick, Karen, Suzanne, and John

Introduction:
The Meaning of Lent

So much has changed in the Catholic Church in recent years. An older generation looks back to a time of tranquility and piety with no hint of any scandal. Now, people almost expect to read in a newspaper or hear from a cable news channel about another failure on the part of church leaders or another criticism by the laity either on the left or on the right.

No one doubts that some things had to change in the church as society changed. With so many changes, however, and as a result of the many church scandals involving sexual misconduct, mismanagement of money, and the abuse of power, people often feel a nostalgia for the simple more stable way of devotions with people praying together or alone, trying to come closer to acknowledging the presence of God in daily life. People need expressions of their faith and ways to express their love of God in a ritual and in prayer.

Lent has always been a time of special prayers and special acts of self-denial. Lent encourages fasting and charity joined with a special awareness of the need to pray. Lent reminds faithful Christians of the price paid for redemption and salvation. During Lent people become more conscious of a failure to accept the gospel message and live it more faithfully.

Throughout These Forty Days We Pray

Lenten devotions offer a possibility for people to express themselves and their needs. Most parishes oblige by offering the opportunity to gather in prayer. People seem to have a hunger for prayer today. People are tired of seeking novelty and have begun to turn to the most important questions of life: *"Does God exist?" "Do I believe in God?" "If so, what kind of a relationship do I have to God?"* When people face these questions, prayer often follows. Only in prayer can a person come to believe in a God and turn to that God in confidence.

Each person has to say his or her own prayers. For centuries the Catholic Church has gloried in a devotional way of the cross. Christians follow in prayer the path of Jesus as he walked through the city of Jerusalem to his death. Believers relive the action of the bystanders. They rekindle in their hearts the appreciation of the suffering of the Lord. They rethink their personal response or even indifference to faith and how easily people can change from proclaiming *"hosanna"* to *"crucify him."*

Following Jesus from Palm Sunday and concluding with the Easter Sunday celebration can lay the foundation for personal Lenten prayer. This prayer demands some study and reading of the Bible. If God has chosen to speak to the human race through this book, then that word of God should be near when people turn to God in prayer. The Bible offers an inexhaustible source for prayer. The Bible consoles in sorrow. The Bible judges when people need to hear a judgment on living. The Bible helps people to grow in faith and trust and in the understanding of that faith and trust.

During Lent the Bible gives a source for meditation, which is always the first step of prayer. In Lent people can relive the ministry of Jesus as recorded in the Gospels. They can examine how they are living as his ministry unfolds and people begin to reject him.

This little book grew out of a series of homilies I preached at St. Thomas More Church in Manhattan in March of 2005 on the Seven Last Words of Jesus. I include additional chapters to fill out the forty days of Lent. During Holy Week the chapters beginning with Palm Sunday and ending with Easter Sunday can be read as preparation for attending the services in church on those holiest of days.

If possible I would urge the reader to read these chapters in church as part of the Lenten practice of praying more in an atmosphere that is conducive for prayer. Of course, a peaceful moment at home can also create the proper environment for reading, thinking, and then perhaps, praying. Clergy may also find these chapters helpful in preparation for preaching during Lent.

The book may also be used for communal devotion. An appendix offers suggestions for a Lenten prayer service in which a leader preaches from the chapters and invites participation.

I extend my gratitude to the Rev. Bernard Kirlin, pastor of St. Augustine Church in Coral Gables, Florida, for reading the manuscript and offering helpful suggestions.

"Throughout these forty days of Lent, we pray."

Miami Shores, Feast of the Sacred Heart, June 3, 2005

I.
Lent Begins

The fundamental motif of Lent involves repentance. The church invites its members to rethink how they are living. *What should stay the same and what should change?* In the different stages of life a person must evaluate and then make some changes.

Temptations change their form as the person changes. Some temptations, however, remain the same with only limited nuances. At different stages in life temptations come and go. How to handle them demands a constant rethinking, a continual effort to repent. The temptations of Jesus offer some helpful hints to everyone.

Each year the Second Sunday of Lent recalls the transfiguration. This marvelous manifestation of the spiritual and the divine through the physical, encourages people not only to recognize the presence of the spiritual in the material, but to allow the spiritual to influence the material.

Throughout the various Sundays in Lent over the three-year cycle, the church offers helpful hints for both repentance and for discovering the spiritual in the midst of the material and the daily aspects of life. Lent involves change, and the Bible gives the guidance for that change.

The voice in the desert.

Repentance

People associate many words, ideas, and attitudes with Lent. The principal word, which includes an attitude, and for many even sums up Lent, is *repentance*. Whenever anyone hears the word, one usually thinks of "sorrow for sins," but the word does not mean that. Certainly repentance involves sin but means rather an attitude in a person that sin can be corrected by changes in the person.

Both the Old Testament and New Testament use the word *repentance,* and in both instances, whether Hebrew *(sub)* or Greek *(metanoia)*, the words connote a turning *(sub)* or a change in mind *(metanoia)*. Since both Testaments suggest a journey in life toward God, repentance is a reexamination of how a person is living and then *turning around,* or changing one's mind and acting differently.

The Old Testament encourages its readers to avoid walking the way of evildoers. Rather, they are to walk the way of the righteous. So when God's people find themselves walking in the way of sinners, they should turn around and walk the right way. Life has its purpose: follow the way of the Lord. When a person deviates, turning around becomes necessary.

Frequently in the Old Testament the authors use the image of an unfaithful bride to describe the people of Israel (Hos 2—3; Jer 15). They have forgotten the love of God, which they experienced in their history, and lived ungrateful to God for their prosperity and good life. They turned away from the way of the Lord to follow the path of the unfaithful. Hosea knows the Lord will never abandon the people and also believes in frequent repentance: "Let us return to the Lord....He will bind up our wounds" (Hos 6:1–2).

Jeremiah has a similar call to return: "Come back to me, apostate Israel, says the Lord" (Jer 3:12). Jeremiah looks for a new heart when the people repent. God will write the Law on their hearts, and they will follow the true path to God. They will return and find comfort in the Lord and in the Law of the Lord. Turning to God involves the heart and not just words. Turning means actions of justice and compassion and mercy and fidelity.

Repentance in Israel also involved a liturgical action. The cultic acts involved symbolic activity such as tearing of garments or wearing coarse garments, putting ashes on the head (Isa 63:7—64:12; Hos 6:1–3, 7:14, 14:1–3; Joel 2:15–18). The actions themselves, however, are meant to symbolize the reality of the change of heart. Otherwise they remain always ritual lies.

Throughout the Psalms the authors call for repentance and promise forgiveness. In particular Psalms 51 and 130 express the meaning of repentance and forgiveness.

READ: Psalm 51 ◆ Psalm 130

Repentance in the Old Testament means changing a way of living and turning to the path that will lead to God.

Repentance means more than empty words. It demands concrete actions of justice, kindness, mercy, compassion, and fidelity: the qualities and virtues associated with the God of Israel.

The New Testament uses the word *metanoia* (change of mind) fifty-four times as a noun and thirty-four times as a verb. Evidently the writers believed the need to change one's mind would characterize following Jesus of Nazareth. The Gospel of John does not use the word, but the other Gospels use the word frequently. John the Baptist in all three Synoptic Gospels calls for a repentance, a change of thinking and then of acting (Matt 3:2; Luke 3:3; Mark 1:4). Jesus follows the same theme as John (Matt 4:17; Mark 1:15). Both arrive on the scene, call for repentance, and eventually are handed over for execution.

Repentance in the New Testament also carries with it a need for faith. Those who believe in Jesus will change their way of living and then experience happiness. In particular Luke 15 and its three parables of the lost sheep, the lost coin, and lost son all have the sense of joy over the one who has repented and changed. The Gospel of Luke ends with a commission: "Repentance and forgiveness of sins will be preached in his name to all the nations" (Luke 24:47).

The Gospel of John does not use the word *repentance* but has the idea of coming to the light. When people move from the darkness and come to the light that is Christ, they have changed their way of living. Then they must remain in the light. At the Last Supper Judas left the room "and it was night" (John 13:30). He turned to darkness.

When Peter preaches in the Acts of the Apostles, people ask what they are to do (Acts 2:37). Peter tells them to "Repent and be baptized" (Acts 2:38). When Paul preaches to the Greeks on the Areopagus, he claims God wants all people to repent (Acts 17:30). Repentance demands first faith and then, with the repentance, sins are forgiven, and people experience the joy of the Lord. People change their way of living; they change their lifestyle.

Conclusion

Repentance in the New Testament always involves rethinking. How easy life would be if people had to do this only once. But repentance is an ongoing process. Regularly, at least once a year in Lent, people who follow Christ must rethink how they are living. They need to reexamine their lifestyle and see what fits and what does not fit. They need to turn first into themselves and then examine the path they are following. They need to evaluate if they have drifted even a little from the path that leads to God through following Jesus. They need to make resolutions and change their actions. People need to think about what they believe and then make sure their activities in life express that faith. People need to repent.

Prayer for Repentance

Compassionate and merciful God,
you invite all who believe to repentance
so that all can find the happiness that all seek.
Help me to trust more in the good news of Jesus
   your Son
so that I can turn my life around,
avoid sin, and live faithful to you and to the
   gospel of the Lord Jesus.
This Lent may I pray more fervently
and listen more attentively to your word.
May my life find transformation by faith in the
   teachings of Jesus.
I make this prayer through Christ our Lord.

Amen.

Jesus goes up to Jerusalem.

Ash Wednesday

In Spanish and Italian Lent is called *Cuaresma* or *Quaresima*, "forty." For more than six hundred years Lent began on the Sunday six weeks before Easter. Early rituals referred to this Sunday as *Quadragesima Sunday*. But since fasting was not allowed on Sunday, to make a complete forty days of fasting four days were added making Lent begin on the Wednesday before the sixth Sunday before Easter.

Originally Lent was a season for repentant sinners to begin to fast and pray in preparation for their readmittance into the community at Easter. Sometime between the eighth and tenth centuries the practice of fasting, prayer, and works of charity extended to the whole community and thus began the current understanding of Lent.

Just as people placed ashes on their heads in the Old Testament time to symbolize repentance, so Christians adopted the same custom. On Ash Wednesday the clergy placed ashes on the heads of the members of the community to signify their willingness to rethink how they were living.

Prayer, fasting, and almsgiving or works of charity form part of the Jewish and Muslim religious traditions as well as Christianity. If people rethink how they are living, they need discipline in their lives and thus the fasting. They need to reconnect with God and thus the prayer, and they need to put into action their belief and thus the works of charity.

Ashes in Judaism and Christianity represent human frailty and weakness as well as mortality. On Ash Wednesday Christians receive ashes with the words: *"Remember man that you are dust and unto dust you shall return"* or *"Repent and believe in the gospel."* The first emphasizes mortality while the second formula recognizes the human weakness in sinning and calls for a rethinking of how a person is living.

In Hinduism ashes represent the pure substance left when the impure substances of life have been removed. Ashes are smeared on the body to symbolize the liberation of the true self from the false self and all that hinders a person from living the true self. This Hindu understanding of ashes can be joined to the Christian understanding since by repentance (symbolized by the ashes) the believer can live a true and authentic Christian life.

Ashes express a desire to rethink. They can express what lives in the heart, or they can be an empty ritual. If a person truly wants to rethink living, that person must think about doing something for the mind, for the body, and for the soul.

READ: Joel 2:12–18 ◆ Psalm 51 ◆
2 Corinthians 5:16–21 ◆ Matthew 6:1–18

The readings for Ash Wednesday call the believer to fast and pray and to give alms. Joel beckons the followers of the Lord to turn to God and to fast, rending hearts and not garments. Joel calls the assembly to gather and to pray, and God will respond with graciousness and mercy.

The responsorial psalm acknowledges sin and asks for mercy. The theme of prayer continues with a hope for the forgiveness of sins and a desire for a clean heart. All involve a new way of living to which God will respond graciously.

The reading from Corinthians calls all to be reconciled with God and experience the joy of God's saving presence. Do not put off reconciliation but do it NOW! Do not delay. Rethink and start acting differently.

Matthew combines prayer, fasting, and almsgiving, the three principal characteristics of Lent. He offers concrete suggestions on how to do each one, avoiding any sense of self-aggrandizement and praise. The church of Matthew early on saw the need for actions to follow beliefs. How a person lives depends on the values the person accepts; for the Christian, those values and beliefs rest on the teachings of Jesus.

Lent will pass quickly. Forty days out of three hundred and sixty-five is meager. True repentance demands action. Believers should do something for their body and in this fasting helps. But taking care of the body through exercise and proper eating belongs to the rest of the year as well as the time of Lent. Lent brings into focus what a follower of Jesus should always be doing.

The human mind needs nourishing. In Lent believers should take care to use and develop the intellectual gifts God has given. Learn something. Read a book; take a class; attend a lecture, but do something to keep the mind active.

The soul also needs to be fed through prayer. Spend some more time in church. Say some extra prayers each day; read the Bible, which combines both mind and soul. Reestablishing a good relationship with God or strengthening that relationship demands time and effort. Lent encourages both.

Conclusion

Lent means rethinking how to live, which involves mind, body, and soul. The days pass quickly. Turn to God and turn thinking into action. Take care of the body, mind, and soul, and then Easter will celebrate new life.

Prayer for Lent
> Grant me, O Lord my God, in this Lent, faith,
>   hope, and love.
> Give me a mind to know you,
> a heart to seek you,
> wisdom to find you,
> and conduct pleasing to you.
> Make me faithful in perseverance, in waiting
>   for you,
> and grant my hope in finally embracing you.
>   Amen.

II.
The Sundays in Lent

The Sundays in Lent present a recurring theme in preparing for both Easter and the celebration of welcoming new converts into the Church at the Easter Vigil. As a time of repentance, each Sunday gives Christians something upon which they may reflect. They read or listen to the readings, reflect upon them, pray as to what the readings may offer, and then take some action that will prepare for Easter.

Thoughtful Christians will decide each Sunday how they can petter prepare for Easter. They will examine their consciences the following Sunday to see how successful they were in fulfilling that decision.

Usually the Lenten season, much like the Advent season, passes quickly. Unless the individual believer takes time to reflect, pray, and act, the season comes and goes, and then Easter arrives without much change in how a person is living his or her life.

Be attentive to what the Word of God has to say. Indeed, it is like a two-edged sword that cuts and heals. This happens, however, only when the person allows the Word of God to affect this or her life.

Damascus•

•Sidon
•Sarepta

•Tyre   •Caesarea Philippi

                    Chorazin
                Capernaum • •Bethsaida
                Gennesaret• *Sea of Galilee*
        Cana •
        Nazareth• Tiberias

MEDITERRANEAN SEA

            •Nain
        •
        Caesarea   •Pella

            •
        Samaria/Sebaste   • Gerasa

    • Joppa
        •Lydda

                    R. Jordan

        •Emmaus

    •Ashkelon
        Jerusalem•
        Bethlehem •

                    Dead Sea
        •Hebron

    Masada •

Beersheba•

                    • Sodom
Map in the time of Jesus.
                    • Gomorrah

The First Sunday of Lent: The Temptations of Jesus

Matthew, Mark, and Luke make reference to the temptations of Jesus, and each Gospel presents them differently. Each Gospel uses the temptations as prelude to the ministry of Jesus. All agree on the place (the desert or a deserted place), the role of the Spirit, and the duration (forty days). The rest of the details differ, even including who did the tempting: the "tempter" in Matthew, "Satan" in Mark, and the "devil" in Luke.

Year A and C:
READ Matthew 4:1–11 ◆ Luke 4:1–13

Matthew focuses on Jesus who experiences an ascetic moment. Here the devil tempts with reverence, and when he leaves, angels comfort Jesus. Neither Matthew nor Luke makes any mention of beasts. Angels do not minister to Jesus in Luke, since for this evangelist, angels minister to God alone. But Matthew and Luke agree on specific temptations, even if they do not agree on the order of the temptations. Both Matthew and Luke make note of the hunger of Jesus. Matthew refers to forty days and forty nights with a possible reference to Moses in Exodus 34:28. Luke's mention of forty days has the notion of completeness.

Both Matthew and Luke agree on the first temptation: turning stones into bread. The second temptation in Matthew, the pinnacle of the Temple, Luke places as the third temptation. The remaining temptation concerns power and wealth. The devil shows Jesus the kingdoms of the world with all of their glory. Jesus triumphs over the devil by winning the rabbinic argument by reciting better scriptural verses. Luke has the better order: bread, power, and tempting God. Since the specific temptations appear only in Matthew and Luke, many think they come from a separate early church document called "Q," a collection of sayings of Jesus.

Since no one witnessed these temptations, some may question how they came to be part of the New Testament. Did Jesus tell his followers what happened, or did an early follower take some sayings from Jesus directed to everyday temptations and arrange them in a way to refer to the power of Jesus over all such human temptations?

The first temptation involves pleasure symbolized by the bread. All pleasure can be tempting whether the pleasure of eating and drinking, or sexual pleasure, or the pleasure of leisure and play. People need pleasure in life, and so Jesus does not condemn pleasure. Not on bread *alone* do people live. Pleasure is good but not the end of all. If people live only for pleasure, pleasure will kill them.

Power, glory, and money also tempt. Jesus teaches to look for power, glory, and honor in the right place: by worshiping God. Christians enjoy the use of money but must use it the right way. Christians worship God by how they take care of each other: "Whatsoever you did to the least of my brethren you did unto me" (Matt 25:40). People who serve others receive power, honor, and glory, and the money seems to be sufficient.

The last temptation in Luke is the most subtle. Throwing oneself off from the pinnacle of the Temple will bring death. God will not save the foolish person. People must learn to accept the consequences of their actions and not blame God or anyone else. Jesus will not tempt God nor should his followers.

Jesus set upon a pinnacle of the Temple.

Year B: READ Mark 1:12–13

Mark's account is the briefest (Mark 1:12–13). The Spirit of God appears as an overpowering force, driving Jesus into the wilderness, a place of loneliness and remoteness, the abode of demons and wild beasts (*theria* = little beasts). The presence of the Spirit highlights the action of God calling and empowering Jesus for this mission. Mark does not mention fasting and makes no reference to any specific temptations. Forty may refer to Moses in Exodus 24:18, Deuteronomy 9:9, or even to Elijah (1Kings 19:8). Forty basically means a sense of completion.

For most Christians Satan is the same as the devil, but not so for the Bible. Old Testament authors frequently personified evil and used many names such as Beelzebul, Beliar, Mastema, or Satan and the devil. Satan originally just meant a tempter and appears in the Book of Job as the accuser in the divine court. In rabbinic literature Satan was the tester or even the executioner of divine judgment. Mark remarks that Jesus experienced temptation, which can come from life as well as from personified evil. Jesus faces the temptations and withstands them with God and angels as witnesses. Then throughout the ministry of Jesus he will confront and will overcome all evil, physical or spiritual. He will overpower the evil that lurks beneath the waves (Mark 4), the illness of paralytics or lepers or the blind (Mark 2–3). He will be with the little beasts *(theria)*, the things "that go bump in the night," and he will triumph over them as well.

Jesus tempted in the wilderness.

Conclusion

Temptations form part of all human life. How one responds to the promptings of mind and heart that cause problems for self and others, makes the difference between saint and sinner or, better, the days when a person lives like a saint and the days in which a person lives like a sinner. People are both. True repentance multiplies the days when temptations become just a part of life rather than a control of life.

Prayer to Resist Temptation

Merciful God, life offers so many temptations:
pleasure for the sake of pleasure, money, power,
and especially the tendency to blame others for
my own failures.
Open my eyes to see the value of pleasure in
my life
to be enjoyed and integrated into living.
Do not let me be blind to the evil use of money
and power.
Above all, help me to accept my failures and try
to remedy them
without seeking to escape responsibility by
blaming others, even you.
I make my prayer in the name of Jesus the Lord.

Amen.

The Second Sunday of Lent: Transfiguration of Jesus

On the Second Sunday of Lent for each year in the three-year cycle people hear the account of the transfiguration of Jesus. The three Synoptic Gospels have the event. The Gospel of John does not record this experience of Jesus with the three apostles. Jesus takes Peter, James, and John to a mountaintop some days after he has responded to the confession of faith by Peter at Caesarea Philippi (Matt 16:13–28; Mark 8:27–9:1; Luke 9:18–27). On the mountain Jesus is transfigured in the presence of his disciples. His clothes shine white; Elijah and Moses appear with him; Peter offers to build tents for each of them to remain; a cloud overshadows them, and a voice speaks from the cloud with the command: "Listen to him." The Master, three disciples, a mountain, a cloud, a vision, and a voice echo what happened to Moses recounted in Exodus 24.

READ Exodus 24

Over the years interpreters have compared this event to resurrection stories, the second coming of Jesus, the heavenly enthronement of Jesus, or the ascension of Jesus. While the event has some similarity to each of these, the event uniquely depicts an important aspect of the life and ministry of Jesus. The event allows the divinity of Jesus to shine through his humanity, and the event contains a heavenly voice that declares divine sonship.

Year A: READ Matthew 17:1–9

Year B: READ Mark 9:2–10

Year C: READ Luke 9:28–36

With the end of prophecy in Israel the people no longer heard the voice of God and often lived with no interest in the concerns of God. The transfiguration hints at the experience of Moses on Mount Sinai and the need for people to hear the voice of God expressed in the material world. Just as God called to Moses from the cloud, so from the cloud God speaks to all present with Jesus, demanding that the chosen three listen to Jesus as the Son of God. Jesus here becomes the new Moses and goes beyond Moses. Then suddenly the theophany ends and they are alone with Jesus. For a moment the divine, the spiritual in Jesus shows forth in the material, the bodily, and the disciples marvel. The bodily, the material remains but now manifests the presence of the spiritual and divine.

The transfiguration might be called the feast of artists since they, more than others, can see the spiritual in the physical. Michelangelo could see a David or a Moses in white marble. Great artists can combine line and color to form masterpieces. Poets can join words together to create beauty as others can join sounds together to create symphonies. All matter can express the spiritual, and thus things need to be cared for. The common everyday elements in life need respect and reverence. Even buildings have a spirituality that is evident when a person visits St. Peter's in Rome or the Capitol building in Washington. Matter does not exist alone but always with spirituality. Spirituality in human experience always needs a physical and human dimension.

Lent calls attention to the body, to the mind, and to the soul. The transfiguration calls to mind the relationship of spirit to matter. One cannot care for the one without the other. The human body expresses the divine; material things have in themselves the presence of the spirit. Recognizing the presence of the spiritual in every aspect of life allows the spiritual to flourish and for human life to blossom.

Transfiguration mosaic.

Conclusion

Everyone has the presence of the spiritual. The human body expresses the spiritual and thus should always be cared for. Everyone is created in the image and likeness of God, having in themselves a spark of the divine, and thus everyone has value and worth and dignity, even if individuals try to destroy this spirituality that they find within.

Prayer for Beauty
The world before me is restored in beauty.
The world behind me is restored in beauty.
The world below me is restored in beauty.
The world above me is restored in beauty.
All things around me are restored in beauty.
It is finished in beauty,
It is finished in beauty,
It is finished in beauty.
—Native American Prayer

Dear and loving God,
Let no one say it and say it to my shame that all
    was beauty here
until I came.

Amen.
—Prayer added by author

The Third Sunday of Lent

Year A: The Samaritan woman

READ John 4:5–42

Throughout the Gospel of John things are not as they appear. Nicodemus was a religious leader who appears in the previous chapter but he does not recognize Jesus as the Messiah. The Samaritan woman, the outsider, and presumably a sinner, does recognize Jesus and becomes an evangelist calling her townsfolk to listen to Jesus.

Jews despised Samaritans and vice versa. The controversy goes back several hundred years. The Samaritans had intermarried with non-Jews; in the eyes of the Jews, they had polluted the bloodline and also seemed to have accepted some religious practices from their neighbors. They had their temple on Mount Gerizim and worshiped God there. Jews would avoid Samaritan territory and would even cross over the mountain to go north from Jerusalem or south from Galilee rather than transverse the territory of the Samaritans. Jesus paid no attention to such practices. He engaged the woman in public in her own territory.

The Samaritan woman was bold and honest. Whether she stands as a symbol of the Samaritan community who had included five foreign gods in their worship or was in fact a woman who had five husbands, makes little difference to the story. She listened, was receptive to what Jesus had to say, and changed her way of living. The woman did not pretend to be other than what she was. Curiosity gave way to final faith, and then she announced Jesus to others.

Water appears throughout this section of the Gospel of John and signifies the presence of the Holy Spirit. Jesus will give this Spirit in his dying. In the seventh chapter the author of the Gospel makes explicit the reference to the Spirit:

If anyone thirst, let him come to me and drink.
He who believes in me, as scripture says,
"Out of his heart will flow rivers of living water."
Now this he said about the Spirit
which those who believed in him were to
    receive.
For as yet the Spirit had not been given
because Jesus was not yet glorified.

John 7:37–39

By asking for the water, the Samarian woman asked for the Spirit. After the resurrection many Samaritans believed in Jesus. They accepted the Spirit. The story involves not just the Samaritan woman but anyone who seeks the Spirit of God.

The woman of Samaria at the well.

All repentance demands honesty, a willingness to listen to the word of the Lord, and then a change in living. Jesus met the woman on her own territory and accepted her as she was. Jesus always acted as such and continues to do so today. The woman's curiosity led to belief. She accepted the Spirit of Jesus and proclaimed him to others.

Year B: Religion means more than observing laws

READ Exodus 20:1–17 ◆ John 2:13–25

People need directions, guidelines, and laws. The Ten Commandments involve relationships with God and with others. If people follow these commands, then people will live in peace; at least such was the theory. Most ancient societies had similar rules of behavior but no ancient society ever lived in peace for an extended time. Laws and commandments are not enough. Too often such laws of behavior degenerate into formal injunctions with some people observing only the minimal without inner conviction and many people ignoring them.

Jesus came not to destroy the Law but to fulfill it. Jesus made it clear that knowing the commandments is not enough. They depend on a personal acceptance of God and others. Laws should express the love of God and love of neighbor. When they do not, they must be ignored.

In the time of Jesus the Law had developed into a complete control of life with regulations affecting every aspect of society. Specific individuals had authority, and the ordinary believer was supposed to accept this authority unquestioningly. Jesus reacted against a sterility of the religion of his day, which too often was content with empty ritual and meaningless regulations. He started by restoring the Temple to a house of prayer. Rules and regulations for offerings were good and necessary, but not when such rules turned the house of the Lord into a marketplace.

The Jews reacted by questioning his authority. Jesus replied with a double-level response. He spoke of the Temple but meant the temple of his body. God dwells in Jesus, not in a building. The Temple reminds people of the presence of God, but in Jesus, God is present to those who will see. Even if people try to destroy this presence, the reality of God in Jesus cannot be denied.

Laws and regulations in Christianity must have their basis in the example of Jesus, who was not limited to the observance of laws. Faith in Jesus, the acceptance of him, forms the heart of the new law, and only with this faith in Jesus and the love of his followers can the church seek to fulfill the Law of God. Relying on laws to bring about repentance brings only failure and frustration. Faith remains primary. Knowing the Ten Commandments and trying to live them is doomed unless the person accepts the heart of the commandments—a belief in God. Knowing God and knowing Jesus brings a freedom in life that goes beyond any law. People of faith fulfill the Law because they live under the care of God with a freedom that exceeds any effort to regulate human life. Jesus fulfilled the Law by how he lived. Christians do likewise.

Year C: People should not try to play God

READ Exodus 3:1–15 ◆ Luke 13:1–9

Religions depend upon a mystical experience of God. Moses had his encounter with God, which caused him to repent, rethink how he was living. After this mystical experience Moses changed his way of living. God charged him with a mission as the father of the Jewish people. It all began with the burning bush.

The actual event matters little. The reaction of Moses and the dialogue with God offer the meaning. In the springtime a bush with bright red flowers and wind blowing the pollen may from a distance look like a burning bush. For Moses, however, it meant the presence of God. Fear and fascination overcame Moses. He recognized the holiness of the moment and place but did not run. He overcame his fear with a calm acceptance of the nearness of God.

In the ancient world, a person's name expressed something of the meaning and nature of the person. Knowing a name gave the knower power over the other. To call a person by name meant intimacy and an entrance into the person's life. It seems Moses wanted to know God more than God was willing to reveal.

Moses asked God his name. God gave an answer that caused bewilderment. Often the Hebrew words (perhaps they are not Hebrew but some other Semitic language) are translated as "I am who I am." But because of the peculiarity of the Hebrew language they also can be translated as "I will be who I will be." Moses wanted to know God in order to control God, and God refused to accommodate Moses. Moses will learn who God is in his own history. Who God is depends upon God, and the meaning of God becomes evident not in knowing a name but in human history, especially the history of the Jewish people.

Christians know more about God than Moses did, for Christians believe that Jesus is God's human face. The mercy and goodness of God become evident in the life, death, and resurrection of Jesus. But still no Christian controls God. No Christian should even think that he or she knows God. The Holy Father chose to put a shell in his coat of arms, reminding himself and others of the story of Augustine and the little boy on the seashore. Just as the boy cannot empty the ocean into the hole in the sand, so neither can Augustine understand God. No one controls God, and so no one should try to play God.

Conclusion

Each reading this Sunday presents some aspect of God as experienced by people. From Exodus, God makes clear that no one can control God nor know God in any complete sense. Both Jesus and Paul speak of the mercy of God, and each demands a response from people of faith.

Prayer for Guidance
Holy God and Father of the Lord Jesus,
open my mind and heart
to be receptive to the teachings of your Son.
Help me to go beyond laws
to live my faith and trust in you.
Let me live lowly in your sight,
always recognizing how much you are beyond me
even as you are with me.

Amen.

The Fourth Sunday of Lent

Year A: God chooses the unlikely

READ 1 Samuel 16:1–13 ◆ John 9:1–41

No one in the time of Saul ever thought the next king would be a shepherd boy. Jesse had a number of sons, and perhaps one of them could be a likely candidate, but the youngest one? Why would God choose him? God does what God wants, and David fitted God's design for Israel. He was a warrior and a poet. The poet in him softened the warrior, and the warrior in him not only accomplished much but also brought strength to the mystical and poetic part of David. And God loved David. David gave glory to God by what he accomplished and eventually in spite of his many sins; he recognized the most important aspect of life is a person's relationship to God.

A blind man also is an unlikely person to give glory to God. Illness came from sin, and surely either a blind person sinned or his parents sinned for God to so punish a person. Jesus says, No! This unlikely person will give glory to God by recognizing the presence of God in Jesus.

Just as the Samaritan woman stands in contrast with Nicodemus, so the blind man contrasts the religious leaders of the Jews. Who really was blind: the religious leaders or the man who could not see? The man born blind sees for he recognizes Jesus for who he is and worships him. Throughout this Gospel Jesus manifests God's grace and truth (John 1:14). Those who truly see, recognize Jesus as God's human face. Those who concentrate only on themselves and their blind ambition, see nothing.

The blind man follows the instructions of Jesus and the water heals him (veiled reference to baptism?). As the water always symbolizes the Spirit of Jesus, the man whom others consider born in sin, allows the water to wash over him, and he becomes a believer anxious to stand up for Jesus in spite

Jesus healing the lame and the blind on the mountain.

of any opposition, even the opposition of the religious leaders. Once again things are other than they appear. The unlikely one, considered a sinner, God chose to give testimony to Jesus. Throughout history God always seems to choose the unlikely, including Jesus.

Year B: God gives freely

Read 2 Chronicles 36:14–23 ◆ John 3:14–21

A true gift comes with no strings attached. The gift symbolizes the giver and should be given in love because of love. A gift not given in love is a bribe. A gift given expecting something in return cheapens the giver. A gift given in hope that it will be used well and appreciated ennobles both the giver and the recipient. People cherish such gifts.

God gives life freely. God attaches no strings to life. God gives in love because of love with the hope that people will appreciate and cherish the gift. God gave life freely, and people can do what they will but also must learn to live with the consequences of their choices.

In the sixth century before Christ the Jews chose to reject the presence of God, and so God abandoned them to their own devices. The suffering of the Babylonian exile resulted from free choice by God's people. But God did not forget the people of Israel but offered them a new opportunity with the coming of Cyrus, king of Persia. God chose Cyrus as the anointed, the messiah, who restored the exiled people to the city of Jerusalem. Centuries passed and again the people suffered from their own decisions, and the city of Jerusalem was again destroyed in the year AD 70. History often seems like a succession of acceptance and rejection of God's gift of life.

God sent Jesus as the final gift, someone in whom people can believe. People need not accept Jesus, need not believe in him; they need not pattern their lives after his example; they need not accept his teaching. God offers a gift and not a bribe. People must freely choose to come to the light, accept the gift of faith, and walk in the light. If some choose to remain in the darkness, such is a free choice and God will not interfere.

The fourth Gospel reminds the readers that judgment is not reserved for a future life, meted out by God alone. People judge themselves and are already judged when they make their basic decisions. Anyone who has come to the light, who has accepted Jesus in faith, has eternal life and need fear no future. The one who flees from the light to hide in darkness is already judged, and the future holds nothing more than the ratification of personal decision. Life is not a series of actions added up in the end to determine reward or punishment. People experience basic orientations in life accepted in freedom because life is God's gift. Basic orientation to God and others influences the details of daily life. People already participate in the future and need not wait for the outcome. Eternal life or eternal death already exists in the days and weeks and years that compile a person's lifetime. God gives freely; people choose freely and then live according to their choices.

Interview between Jesus and Nicodemus.

Living in freedom with the possibility of accepting or rejecting God often frightens. Some would like to hand over all power of decision to others or to rules and regulations or a conduct of life that promises a reward if carefully observed. Life might be simpler if such a process would be possible, but if life is a personal gift, then no one can hand this gift to another to be ruled and controlled. Each person must stand in the presence of God and acknowledge how the gift was accepted. No pope, priest, friend, book, or law can take that place. In freedom people judge themselves. God ratifies personal choice. People either enter into eternal life with God because they have already lived with God, or they will turn to darkness and despair because darkness and despair has already been their chosen lot.

Year C: To reconcile means to unite what was separated

READ Joshua 5:9–12 ◆
2 Corinthians 5:17–21 ◆ Luke 15:1–32

Reconciliation sounds familiar enough to most Roman Catholics especially since for the past forty years they have heard about the sacrament of reconciliation rather than the sacrament of penance. The reality, however, may be far from a frequent experience. God reconciles and then begins the work of people. The former can always be presumed; the latter often seems to be lacking.

In this Sunday of Lent each reading deals with reconciliation. During the long years in the desert the Jewish people failed often in their promises to their God. When Joshua led the people across the Jordan, he proclaimed a day of rededication for all the people. During the desert period the rite of circumcision had been neglected, even though this had previously been the principal sign of the relationship between God and the people. With the ceremony of rededication the males were circumcised, and the "reproach of Egypt" mentioned in the reading from Joshua was removed. God was present to the people seeking reconciliation. The people had to join in this action by moving toward God's presence and promising fidelity.

Paul also emphasizes the divine role in reconciliation. Through Jesus God has shown his face, a countenance of mercy and forgiveness. The world had been alienated from God, and now through Jesus God has reunited all of creation. God will not count sins against the people but extends an offer of peace. God has taken the initiative and has accomplished what God proposed. Now God has given to the church a similar mission of continuing the ministry of reconciliation. The barriers that separate people are broken; the obstacles that prevent a peaceful life for people are removed. People are no longer separated within and without. God has done something good and calls people to continue the mission of uniting all people together with God.

The parable of the prodigal son appears only in the Gospel of Luke. Often this fifteenth chapter is called "the gospel within the gospel" for it expresses in a clear fashion the meaning of God and God's relationship to creation: forgiveness and reconciliation.

God attaches no strings to the gift of life. If an individual chooses to dissipate his or her life, one is free to do so and God does not interfere. The parable has one meaning: the mercy and compassion of God when a sinner returns and accepts reconciliation. The divine quality becomes more evident in contrast with the attitude of the older brother who does not wish to share in the joy of the father in the returning brother. The parable presents in story form the greatness of divine compassion and how far removed God's mercy stands in relationship to human forgiveness.

The reconciliation presented in the parable does not emphasize the action of the father moving toward the son. First the son has to return on his own; he must acknowledge his need and come determined to seek reconciliation. Once the son resolves to seek the reconciliation with the father, the father does not wait for the prepared speech but envelops the son in a loving embrace of forgiveness. The movement begins with the son, but the father does not wait for its completion but anticipates the final reconciliation.

Reconciliation presupposes the presence of God and concludes with the acceptance by God. But the action must be initiated by the one who has chosen to walk away. God will not force anyone but will allow people to live their own lives even when that living is not in accord with the will of God. God also places reminders in the paths of all people calling for a return. God's presence is powerful and may even entice people to overcome their alienation and separation.

Conclusion

On the human level, people take the initiative to be reconciled with others and like God give support to those who have deliberately chosen to turn away. The goal remains the same: people united in peace dwelling under a provident God. "We implore you in Christ's name to be reconciled to God" through a reconciliation with one another.

Prayer for Living Well in Freedom

God, you have chosen me and blessed me with
the gift of life.
I will never understand why you have so
blessed me.
I live my own life, and you support me
no matter what I do or fail to do.
Help me to live my freedom well
and continually seek to be united
with you through Christ your Son.

Amen.

The Fifth Sunday of Lent

Year A: Eternal life has begun

READ Ezekiel 37:12–14 ♦ John 11:1–45

Many people have experienced hell on earth. Whether natural disasters or acts of terrorism or cataclysmic pain and suffering, some people have known the terrible torture of separation and agony and lived in the midst of despair tearing away any desire for life. For some the only answer to such an experience is ending life. Even in the midst of such pain, what a waste!

Ezekiel, who lived through the terrible hell of exile and separation and apostasy on the part of many people, lived with a hope for the future. Priest and noble, he lost all but not his commitment to God and his hope for future restoration, even if he probably never lived to see the return to the land of Israel. For Ezekiel heaven meant a hope for the future.

If hell begins on earth so does heaven. The Gospel of John concentrates not on present or future pain but on present glory. Lazarus had died, but on hearing the word of Jesus

Tomb of Lazarus.

he returned to life. God has power over death, and since Jesus is the human face of God, Jesus has power over death.

By the time this Gospel was written (around AD 90–95) many followers of Jesus had died, yet he had not returned. Some Christian preachers pushed the coming of Jesus into the distant future. The Gospel of John brings the future into the present. Eternal life has begun: "this is eternal life: to know the one true God and Jesus Christ whom he has sent" (John 17:3). "He who hears my word and believes in him who sent me has eternal life; he does not come into judgment but has passed from death to life" (John 5:24). "I am the resurrection and the life; the one believing in me, even if he should die, will live, and anyone living and believing in me by no means dies" (John 11:25–26).

Heaven has begun for those who believe. They need fear no future judgment, for they have made their decision to come to the light. On earth they will experience troubles, "but be of good cheer; I have overcome the world" (John 16:33). Anyone who has heard the word of Jesus and has come to the light can always count on moments of experiencing the presence of God. Heaven has begun when life seems good and someone sends a thank-you note or flowers, or in the springtime after a long winter, or when we are enjoying a family meal or seeing the Grand Canyon or listening to music. Heaven on earth means moments of experiencing the presence and goodness of God, and those moments are always there, even in the midst of what seems like hell.

Martha and Mary believed, and Lazarus heard the words of Jesus and Lazarus was alive. Better to concentrate on the heavenly moments to be able to deal with the hellish moments.

Year B: What is the purpose of life?

READ Jeremiah 31:31–34 ◆ John 12:20–33

Where is love? What is life's purpose? What does life mean? When asking these questions, the person is facing adulthood and maturity. The rich young man in the Gospel went to Jesus when he was troubled with the meaning of his life; Jesus told him to lose his life for the sake of finding it. Give up all and follow Jesus if you wish to find the answer to the riddle of life.

The Gospel of John goes further: unless the grain of wheat dies, it does not bring forth life. But what does it mean to die, to lose one's life, to hate one's life in order to find it? Finding meaning and purpose in life demands a willingness to overcome selfishness and pride and freely give of oneself to Jesus and to his gospel.

Finding life in death seems odd if not absurd. Some will simply say that the follower of Jesus must share in the sacrifice of Jesus who died to his own will in his acceptance of the will of God. And he died to himself in his faithful love of others. At least in some sense dying while living involves an acceptance of the will of God, no matter how difficult or how confusing, and a living for the sake of others.

In the past Catholics found it somewhat easy to discover the will of God since it was identified with church law and practice, as well as the commands of those who were leaders in the church. Today this does not work. Even the ascetical practices that promised to help in discovering the will of God have fallen by the wayside. And popes and bishops seem reluctant to identify themselves so easily with the will of God, especially with the failure on the part of many church leaders. What once was easy to know has become harder to discover today.

The Bible offers some suggestions. People need to make room for God in their lives. This means prayer. To die to oneself involves an awareness of someone beyond the self, beyond the ordinary aspects of human daily life. Dying to self forces a person to acknowledge the presence of God in life.

Jesus gave of himself to his friends and even to his enemies. The crucifixion alone is not the sacrifice of Jesus. Calvary culminated his life of giving to others. He lived doing good for others. That also involves a dying to oneself. To die to oneself, to share in the sacrifice of Jesus, to be filled with the Spirit of Jesus means to open oneself to others. Being kind and considerate or even polite when people do not repay the compliment causes a dying to oneself. Service offered often causes pain since it is offered at the expense of the giver, and some people actually resent the offer.

Lent also reminds Catholics of their commitment to the poor and anyone in need. Unfortunately in American society that usually means a check. Giving of time and talents and sharing others' burdens better respond to those in need. Moreover, if anyone tries to offer a piece of bread to the poor and that bread is not covered with love, the poor will choke on it and the giver will suffer as well.

Life comes through dying to self for the sake of God and others. Too often people are afraid of losing what they already have, but if a person opens himself or herself and makes room for God and for others in life, then the person does not lose but gains.

Year C: God is compassionate to all

READ Isaiah 43:16–21 ◆
Philippians 3:8–14 ◆ John 8:1–11

God continues to create something new. The past never need be the measure of the future. No one should ever feel condemned to relive the mistakes of the past or to be falsely bound to the imperfections and sins of days gone by. As long as a person lives, the person has hope and expectations and great possibilities.

Isaiah knew God for he had experienced the power of God to make things new. The desert would blossom; rivers would flow freely; people would drink and be refreshed. The Lord God would do it all because of the great love of God for the people of Israel. God would forget the past, and the people of God could stand and face the future with assured confidence.

Paul also experienced the power of God. He did not first choose God, but God chose him. He did not possess God, but God possessed him. The power of the resurrection of the Lord filled his person, creating a dynamic tension pulling him into the future and bringing with him all those who would listen to his preaching. He used the image of a runner in a race whose eyes remain riveted on the finish line. Paul would continue to run toward the future prize, taking with him vast throngs of people who had become believers because of his preaching. The new thing that God had accomplished became the pulsating force in the life of Paul, and all else meant nothing.

Paul saw the expectations: a prize worth dying for and worth living for. The future had begun, and now he was continually being drawn into the circle of God finally to be enveloped by God alone. Paul could look back to Isaiah and know in his heart that the desert of human life was indeed in blossom and water was cascading, giving refreshment to all who wanted it. Forgiveness would characterize human experience; compassion would be the hallmark that God had chosen to offer to people grown tired of what seemed to be eternally old. "Behold, I am doing something new" is not limited to the time of Isaiah nor to the time of Jesus or Paul. God does new things for people now. Open your eyes to see.

The woman taken in adultery placed Jesus in a dilemma. The Law called for stoning, but Jesus ignored the Law to show the new thing that God had created in history through Jesus: forgiveness and compassion are God's qualities, and these will be manifest. The leaders of the Jews knew that Jesus taught compassion, but to teach that theoretically would cause no problem; on the other hand, the teacher with the freedom to live as he taught would undermine the moorings of religious society. Faced with a violation of Mosaic Law, would the teacher be subject to the Law and faithful to its teaching, or would he be faithful to his own teaching or, finally, would he try to hedge and protect himself? Would the new thing that was Jesus of Nazareth really be something very old and only appear to be new? Would the deserts of human life really blossom, and would water refresh the soul of the sinner?

"Let him who is without sin cast the first stone." The woman need not be condemned to the past. The future was important and not the sins of a previous life. God, through Jesus, does offer something new and not just to those who are righteous but to all peoples of all times. Since her accusers quietly slipped away, no one remained to bear witness against her. Neither would Jesus. The new thing that God had begun in Jesus was truly new, unlike anything that had preceded it. The compassionate God had been manifest in Jesus. Jesus lived a human life in which the divine was made evident.

Conclusion

The word of God continues to offer something new. Once God began this new thing in Jesus, God has not stopped offering. Christianity is the assurance that no one person should feel condemned to the past; all of us are open to a future beyond the most wild of expectations. Hopes and desires are fulfilled not in an incomplete way but in a way surpassing human imagination.

Prayer for Hope
>   Lord God, sometimes the burdens of life seem
>   so heavy
>   that I do not have the courage to be.
>   I see too much sadness and pain; I know anger
>   and resentment.
>   I do not fear hell for I have been in it.
>   Help me to recognize your presence; give me a
>   taste of heaven now.
>   Do something new for me for I am in need.
>   I make my prayer, confident of your compassion
>   and love.
>   Amen.

Palm Sunday

READ: Matthew 21:1–11 or Mark 11:1–10 or
Luke 19:28–40 or John 12:12–16
and Matthew 26:17—27:54 or
Mark 14:12—15:39 or Luke 22:1—23:49

The Liturgy of Palm Sunday has two gospels: the gospel of the triumphant entrance of Jesus into Jerusalem and the gospel of the passion of Jesus. In the three-year cycle of readings, each of the Synoptic Gospels (Mark, Matthew, and Luke) is read on a rotating basis. The Gospel of John is read on every Good Friday.

In the celebration of the liturgy, the followers of Jesus move from a glorious acceptance of Jesus to the call for his death. How quickly people change their minds! In some ways, it is good that people can change since no one need feel condemned to the mistakes of the past, but people can also move from the good and true and lovely to embrace the sordid, the ugly, and the perverse. On Palm Sunday the liturgy reminds people of how quickly they can change from acknowledging Jesus as Messiah to asking for his crucifixion. How fickle people are! Those followers of Jesus succumbed to the temptation to espouse a cause without personal involvement. Today no one should feel innocent of such fickleness since followers of Jesus quickly proclaim him as Savior and Son of God and then reject him and his gospel by personal sin.

The narrative of the death of Jesus is the oldest part of all of the Gospels. His death was difficult to explain, and so the early preachers would have carefully narrated what had happened as they prepared people to accept the resurrection. The death and resurrection of Jesus was the heart of the earliest preaching and was the first section of his gospel to reach a written form.

Jesus had to suffer before he died. Three times in each of the Synoptic Gospels Jesus predicts his passion and death. In both Mark and Matthew he cries out, "My God, my God, why have you forsaken me?" For each Gospel the rejection of Jesus and his passion and death create a great tragedy in human history. Humankind has said "No" to goodness. But God will not allow goodness to be destroyed. Even with the passion and suffering, Jesus will triumph in his resurrection.

Why did Jesus have to die? Why did Jesus have to die a cruel death on the cross? Certainly if Jesus was human in every sense but without sin, then he had to die just as every human being has to die. Jesus had to experience the darkness and separation associated with death. But why the crucifixion?

People tend to destroy what is good. Good embarrasses and so often it seems easier to destroy or belittle or deny the goodness rather than allow the goodness to influence thought and behavior. The death of Jesus is the supreme manifestation of the human refusal to allow goodness to heal and overcome evil. The crucifixion brings to conclusion the power of evil that began in Genesis in original sin. Sin multiplied itself with the human race rejecting the great gift of God, Jesus of Nazareth. God changed this sign of human folly into a sign of redemption and eternal love.

Jesus lived and died in love and obedience to God his Father. His fidelity resulted in his resurrection and his coming as Messiah in power, capable of giving his Spirit. The darkest hour of human history became, by the power of the love of God, the beginning of human glory. People can now live by the Spirit of Jesus because Jesus lived and died and was raised. The reversal of the power of evil has begun. Evil meets goodness; rejection encounters love and acceptance; forgiveness overcomes hatred. The new dawn has begun.

Conclusion

People should feel a little sadness during Holy Week, and Palm Sunday's liturgy offers a good opportunity. People still say "No" to goodness. People still ridicule others who are good. People still pick out the negative in others even in those they love. Why not celebrate the goodness in others? Why not emphasize the positive? Feel sad for a moment, but then think of all that God has given to the human race and celebrate the goodness of life.

Prayer for Daily Guidance

Good and gracious God,

You have a great and loving plan for the world
and for me.

Help me to accept and celebrate all that is good
in life.

Guide me to avoid all evil and all that is
negative.

By your gift of the Spirit, make my sadness give
way to joy.

May I bask in the sure hope of a good future

since you have already blessed me in the past in
Jesus your Son.

Amen.

III.
The Seven Last Words of Jesus

The ancient Catholic practice of meditating on the Seven Last Words of Jesus raises a level of awareness of the last hours in the life of the Lord. No one Gospel has all of the words, and only one of the words appears in more than one Gospel. These final words of Jesus run the gamut from darkness to light and care for others and confidence in God. They belong in any Lenten effort to grow in faith and repentance and reconciliation.

Traditionally these Seven Last Words formed the subject of meditation during the hours from noon to three on Good Friday. They may form part of a personal meditation at any time or place during Holy Week, including time spent in preparation for the Good Friday Service of the Word and reception of the Eucharist.

The First Word: "Father, forgive them, for they know not what they do" Luke 23:34

Most people like the Gospel of Luke. In this Gospel the evangelist portrays Jesus as the kind and compassionate Savior. Jesus has a special care for the outcasts, the marginalized, the downtrodden, the poor, and the oppressed. Jesus reaches out to all who are lost from God, especially those who feel as if the world and society have forgotten them. Jesus forgives and pardons.

This Gospel contains one of the favorite parables: the prodigal son. In the fifteenth chapter, Luke also includes two other parables that are proper to Luke; the parable of the lost sheep and the parable of the lost coin. The kind and compassionate Jesus reaches out to those in need and forgives.

It is not surprising that the first words of Jesus from the cross are words of forgiveness. Jesus will hold no grudges. He will not condemn anyone. He knows too well the weakness of the human heart and the proclivity of people to destroy that which is good, even a good person such as Jesus. With forgiveness in his heart, Jesus turns to God, his Father, and asks God to forgive those who have brought him to the cross.

"Father," such a tender word. The Aramaic means more than the formal English word *father*; it carries a sense of intimacy and familiarity. Jesus knows God in a personal and intimate way and also knows God will not deny his request. It is so hard for anyone to envision what God is really like. Jesus as God's human face reveals God and informs his followers that God is like a kind and loving parent anxious to listen to the prayers of all. If people can think of the best qualities of their mothers and the best qualities of their fathers, and combine them, then they can understand something of what God is like: a kind and loving parent. Jesus turns to this kind and loving Father and prays not for himself but for others.

So often people think that those responsible for the death of Jesus lived in the first century. Some Romans and some Jews killed Jesus. In fact, anyone who has destroyed anything that is good contributed to the death of Jesus. The crucifixion in the words of Karl Barth is the human "no" to goodness. People tend to destroy what is good, and Jesus was a good man. People put down those who are good, for good people remind other people of what they could and should be. Putting someone down makes it easier to live with oneself.

"She is such a good person who gives so much to the church, but she does not take care of her kids!" "He helps everyone in the neighborhood, but he drinks too much!" People destroy people and people tried to destroy Jesus. Yet, he asks for forgiveness for them and thus for all who tend to destroy what is good. The "them" in these words of Jesus applies to everyone in the church. Jesus asks God to forgive even his followers for what they do when they destroy others.

Crucifixion is a terrible way to die. Usually the person dies of asphyxiation. The weight of the body hanging from the cross makes it difficult to breathe and then impossible to breathe. Very often people concentrate on the nails through hands and feet. How excruciatingly painful must that have been. The physical pain especially after viewing Mel Gibson's *Passion of the Christ* seems to be beyond what a human being can bear. And yet, Jesus bore the pain for three hours.

In addition to the physical pain, the shame of crucifixion added to the torture. In Christian art Jesus is given some dignity with a cloth around his waist. In reality no such reverence was given to the crucified.

Anyone who has had the misfortune of being in a hospital for tests or an operation knows how quickly all human dignity is lost with the little hospital gowns. How humiliating to be fully exposed in public.

Some years ago while in Jerusalem an American visitor lived in a religious institute between Jerusalem and Bethlehem. One May day, since it was very warm he walked down into Bethlehem wearing shorts. How dumb could he have been! An Arab man would never appear in public with shorts. They have a profound sense of modesty and reverence for the human body. Once he realized what he was doing by the looks on the faces of the men in Bethlehem, he quickly took a taxi home. Imagine how many Arab men felt as they saw the pictures of the Abu Ghraib prison in Iraq!

Poor Jesus was tortured physically as well as psychologically and emotionally. Those people two thousand years ago did a terrible thing to a human being, and Jesus asks forgiveness for them!

Conclusion

If God forgives all who have hurt others, then true repentance demands a change in living. Too easily people pick out what is wrong with others. How much better to pick out what is right. When someone says something good about another person, then add to the remarks by adding to the expression of goodness. If someone says something bad about another, try to think of something good about the same person. And if anyone says something bad about you, then forgive as you have been forgiven and your forgiveness will be complete.

Prayer for Truthfulness
>Keep me, O Lord, from all pettiness.
>Let me be large in thought, in word and in deed.
>Let me be done with fault finding and leave off
>all self-seeking.
>May I put away all pretenses and meet others
>face to face
>without self-pity and without prejudice.
>Grant that I my realize that it is the little things
>in life
>that create differences.
>And, O God, let me never forget to be kind.
>
>Amen.
>
>—*Mary Stewart*

The Second Word: "Truly I tell you, this day you will be with me in paradise" Luke 23:43

The kind and compassionate Jesus in the Gospel of Luke first sought for forgiveness for all those who had led him to the cross. He held no grudges. He did not lash out against anyone. He turned to a forgiving father and pleaded for others. His second word also from the Gospel of Luke offers kindness and compassion and hope to the thief at his side.

The Gospels say two criminals were crucified with Jesus. Rome regularly crucified a number of victims together. Luke says they were criminals. Matthew and Mark say they were robbers (Matt 27:38; Mark 15:27). John merely mentions that two were crucified with Jesus (John 19:18). Who were these criminals, robbers? Were they common criminals or zealots anxious for the overthrow of Rome? What exactly did they do to deserve such a punishment?

One thief recognizes Jesus for who Jesus is. He asks to be remembered when Jesus enters into his kingdom. The Old Testament has a long history of understanding the reign of

God. The people had known too much the reign of earthly kings with all of their pettiness and abuse of power. The people of Israel longed for the reign of God. The Messiah would come, and he would reign as God wanted and not as royalty wanted. The birth of each new prince brought a hope that perhaps this would be the desired Messiah, the anointed one of God who would reign on earth as God reigned in heaven. And each time hope gave way to despair as the young prince grew and became like all of the others before him.

If only the Messiah would come and reign and bring a rule of justice—harmony and balance. If only the Messiah would come to bring peace to the people of Israel when each man and woman could wish only the best to their fellow believers. If only the Messiah would come to bring the love that binds people together caring for each other. If only the Messiah would come to bring freedom from oppression and neglect and want. Then the reign of God would be on earth as it is in heaven.

Whatever the person crucified with Jesus had done, he recognized Jesus as the Messiah who would inaugurate the reign of God, and he wanted to be part of it.

Throughout his life Jesus aligned himself with the bad elements, the sinners, the tax collectors, and the prostitutes. He died numbered among the transgressors (Isa 53:12). Jesus was not sacrificed on an altar between two candles but on Calvary between two thieves, men of violence. Jesus was not numbered among the pillars of religious society for only bad elements in society were crucified. If they had white collar crimes in those days, and surely they did, if these criminals were punished they suffered much like white collar criminals today and not by crucifixion. Jesus was crucified outside the walls of the city. The holy city wouldn't be contaminated by the death of such evildoers.

One thief taunts Jesus. "If you are the Messiah, save yourself and us!" Evidently some had said that Jesus was the Messiah, and so one of the thieves mocks Jesus. The other recognizes the proper fate of the two thieves and asks to be remembered.

People do not like Good Friday. It is too gruesome, too much like the depiction in Mel Gibson's *Passion of the Christ*. More people come to Mass on Easter than attend services on Good Friday. Easter is good and tasteful while Good Friday is ugly. Jesus dying with two thieves is not a pretty picture. But not both thieves are ugly, and Jesus, even if as ugly as Gibson depicts him, is still the divine Son of God, the Messiah who will bring about the reign of God. One thief recognizes all of this and wants to be remembered in the kingdom.

To remember in the Bible is not just thinking, but actually doing something. When God remembers, God acts. The good thief does not want Jesus to think nice thoughts about him but to do something for him. He wants a biblical remembrance and that means being part of the kingdom. He wants to belong and asks Jesus to be sure to make him a part of it.

Conclusion

At times everyone in the church acts like the bad thief. They want Jesus to do something for them. Show your power; give some shock and awe so all can really change their way of living. "If you are the Messiah, show it!"

And at times everyone in the church is like the good thief. They know their sins, they have suffered justly. They recognize Jesus as the Messiah even if he has no outward signs of power and glory. They believe in his kingdom whose foundation is justice for all, a balance and harmony that unites all people. A kingdom where love is the rule and peace, wishing good to all, is the mandate in an atmosphere of complete freedom. They believe in such a kingdom and want to be remembered so they can share in this reign.

Everyone can ask Jesus for remembrance: *"Remember me, Lord, when you come into your kingdom."*

Prayer for the Kingdom
Let justice, balance, and harmony surround me.
Let freedom protect me.
Let love support me.
Let peace be within me for peace is your gift to me.
Then, O God, all is well.

Amen.

The Third Word: "Son, behold thy mother; Woman, behold thy son"
John 19:27

Over the centuries these words have been interpreted to show the care that Jesus had for his mother. In the third century Augustine listened to these words and recognized the concern that Jesus had for his mother's future now that he would no longer be present to help her. While Jesus was dying, he thought of her welfare. In the midst of his pain and loss he wanted the Beloved Disciple to take care of his mother. Surely, then, all of the followers of Jesus should take care of their mothers.

Augustine himself had a turbulent relationship with his mother, Monica. She shed many tears for her wayward son, hoping and praying that he would come to his senses, become a Christian, and be baptized. At one point she turned to St. Ambrose and poured out her heart concerning her son. Ambrose responded: "The child of so many tears will never be lost." When Augustine did turn from his wayward life, no wonder he could read these verses and think of his own mother and know the sorrow he had caused her.

As pleasant as this interpretation seems, it does not do justice to the Gospel of John. The Mother of Jesus appears only twice in this Gospel: here at the foot of the cross and at the marriage feast of Cana. In both instances Jesus calls her Woman. The Gospel never mentions her name, Mary. It sounds strange for a son to call his mother Woman. Certainly it lacks any sense of affection and warmth. The very use of the term should immediately alert the reader that something else is going on here. In the fourth Gospel the Mother of Jesus as well as the Beloved Disciple are not only historical figures; they are symbolic figures who have, by virtue of their position in the Gospel, another dimension.

The Greek text concludes with the words: "he took her to his own that very hour." Some have interpreted this to mean that the Beloved Disciple took her to his home. Today visitors to Ephesus can see the home where the Beloved Disciple was supposed to have taken Mary although no historical evidence exists to support this position. The meaning of the words of Jesus has to do more with the relationship within the church than with the historical circumstances of Mary and the Beloved Disciple.

This word from the cross by Jesus has nothing to do with Jesus being concerned with the welfare of his mother, nor does it mean that we should all take care of our mothers, however admirable this might be. Rather the word of Jesus concerns the new community that comes into being through the death of Jesus. In this Gospel, as Jesus dies, the author says, "And bowing his head he handed over his spirit." Again, over the years many have translated these Greek words in different ways. The old English version translated as "and bowing his head he gave up the ghost" seemed to mean that he died. But the word *hand over* is important in the New Testament. From it we get the word *tradition,* something that has been passed on from one generation to another. Here Jesus passes on his spirit to the two perfect disciples at the foot of the cross: his mother and the Beloved Disciple. In the Gospel of John the church is born at Calvary and not at Pentecost. The new community of the Mother of Jesus and the Beloved Disciple creates the new community of faith and Spirit-filled people able to carry on the ministry of Jesus.

Very often today many will say they do not need to go to church to experience God. Going to the mountains or especially the ocean can bring a sense of the divine. Others say they can be a follower of Jesus without being part of a church community. Both groups miss the power of the community of faith. In an age of support groups for every need it is strange that some do not see the need for a support group of faith. In New York after 9/11 the support of family and friends continues to help those left behind cope with their loss. People need people in life. The same is true for people of faith.

When the institutional church has been racked with scandal, some ask why bother? Yet, when the Christian community functions as it should as a community of faith and Spirit-filled people supporting each other in spite of the sins and failures, even of religious leaders, then Christianity has a power that will conquer the world. All this began on Calvary when Jesus gave his mother to the Beloved Disciple and the Beloved Disciple to his mother.

The unnamed Woman and the unnamed disciple represent the way that family ties are no longer important in the family of Jesus. Everyone is welcome. In the words of Paul: "There is neither Jew nor Greek, slave nor free, male and female; but we are all one in Christ Jesus" (Gal 3:28).

Conclusion

Jesus calls his mother Woman to set aside the blood relationship to create a family of faith. The words are addressed to everyone in this church today. Look at the person on your right and on your left. They are your family. The people in front and behind are your family. The words of Jesus do not mean that his followers should care for their mothers, but that his followers should care for each other. If you believe that God cares for you, if you believe that Jesus cares for you, then you are capable of caring for someone else, especially your own mother but not limited to your mother. The old expression "Charity begins at home" takes on a special meaning as members of the community of faith care for each other.

"Woman, behold thy son; Son, behold thy mother." Jesus addresses his community in the church today.

Prayer: The Memorare

> Remember, O most compassionate Virgin Mary,
> That never was it known
> That anyone who fled to your protection,
> Implored your help, or sought your intercession
>   was left unaided.
> Inspired by this confidence,
> I fly unto you, O virgin of virgins, my mother.
> To you do I come; before you I kneel sinful and
>   sorrowful.
> O mother of the Word Incarnate, despise not my
>   petitions
> But in your clemency hear and answer me.
>
>   Amen.

The Fourth Word:
"My God, my God, why have you forsaken me?"
Mark 15:34, Matthew 27:46

How could God have forsaken Jesus? Jesus was the faithful, loyal divine Son. He had lived a life of service to others. He had accomplished the will of God, and now God has forsaken him? Hard to believe.

Over the centuries Christians have been troubled by this word from the cross. It could not be true. Jesus could not have felt abandoned by God. God could not have left Jesus alone. And so some said he was reciting the Psalm. Yet this is the only word from the cross that appears in two Gospels, Mark and Matthew. Since Matthew had Mark as a source, maybe he just copied it. But Luke also had Mark as a source and did not include this word in his Gospel. If Matthew included it from Mark, he must have felt it belonged.

In the Gospel of Mark the family of Jesus thinks he is crazy (Mark 3:21). The religious leaders accuse him of being in league with the devil (Mark 3:22), and his disciples do not understand him. Jesus experienced rejection, vile accusation. He was misunderstood, not appreciated. He knew all of the ordinary bad experiences of being left alone, put on the periphery of society, marginalized, and in his final moments thought God had joined in and abandoned him.

Life is filled with light and wonder and happiness and joy. Unfortunately life also has its darkness and separation, and with death a person experiences the final separation and darkness. Is there anyone there? Does anyone care? Is there a kind and compassionate God or only emptiness and eternal darkness? Is death the end of a bad dream called living, or is death the doorway to a life of never-ending joy? Can anyone experience the warmth of the elixir of life without also knowing the pit of despair?

Johann Sebastian Bach wrote his *St. Matthew Passion* and surrounded the words of Jesus with a halo of string music. It adds a flourish to the words of Jesus. But there are no happy strings around these words in Bach's *Passion*. Jesus is alone.

People are afraid of dying. For some, death comes as an invited guest, but that usually happens only after a long period of pain and suffering. Life is precious and no one wants to rush to give it up. If they do, that is a sure sign of deep psychological and spiritual trouble. Life is meant to be lived even on bad days. But the time comes when death is at the door and then the person must face death alone.

The image of a person dying surrounded by loved ones is comforting. Unfortunately nine out of ten people die alone. The body no longer can support the life-giving spirit.

Age or accident or the ravages of illness have taken away from the body the ability to express the spiritual dimension of the human person. Life, as we know it, is ended.

> To sleep—perchance to dream. Aye, there's
>   the rub,
> For in that sleep of death what dreams may
>   come
> When we have shuffled off this mortal coil,
> Must give us pause. *Hamlet* III, i, 65–68

Death comes to all living creatures, and all living things die reluctantly. The plant dying of thirst will hang on with the hope of being revived. The dying animal will writhe in agony. The human being possesses the highest level of life and has the most to lose. The death of a person must, however, differ from the death of animal and plant. Everyone here knows that he or she will die. Animals and plants die as well. But people do not want to die. People want to live without end. The necessity of dying and the lack of full understanding confound human reason and make death a theme frequently avoided while at the same time the subject of inexhaustible treatment.

Death involves action and suffering, a surrender of the bodily form and a beginning of an all-cosmic relationship of spirit. Death means an end of the biological and the consummation of the personal life from within.

The death of Jesus was redemptive. By it the value, the worth, the goodness given to every human being by God by being created in the image and likeness of God, will be preserved eternally. Jesus suffered death as the expression and the manifestation and the revelation of sin in the world. He did so in absolute liberty as the act and the revelation of the divine grace, which rendered divine the life of his humanity.

Precisely in its darkness the death of Jesus becomes the expression and the incarnation of his loving obedience, the free offering of his entire created existence to God. Through the death of Jesus his spiritual reality that he possessed from the beginning, enacted in his life, and brought to consummation in his death becomes open to the whole world and is inserted into this world as a permanent destiny of all.

Conclusion

Jesus had to experience the darkness and the separation that we all will experience. He had to trust God but first he had to feel as if he was truly alone and abandoned. In that experience he could then say, "Father, into your hands I commend my spirit."

Prayer for Preparing for Death

> Lord and God of all, lead me from death to life,
> From falsehood to truth.
> Lead me from despair to hope,
> From fear to trust,
> From hatred to love.
> Let peace fill my heart and my world.
>
> Amen.

The Fifth Word:
"I Thirst" John 19:28

A crucified and dying person thirsts. I suppose no one could possibly know the pain of wanting water and receiving nothing. The human body needs water to survive. We can survive for a long period of time without food but not without water.

Most Americans drink good water. Few people in the United States have known extreme thirst. In most of the developed world water is just taken for granted. Even drought in parts of the West does not mean that people do not have water to drink. Civilized people have abundance of water and too often waste it. In underdeveloped countries water is more valuable than gold. You cannot drink gold.

Just before he dies, according to the Gospel of John, Jesus says "I thirst." Given that a crucified person would have become dehydrated, especially after the scourging, the nailing to the cross, and the hanging in agony, "I thirst" makes sense. Jesus wanted some water.

But this meaning does not do justice to the theology of the Gospel of John. Each word from the cross by Jesus supports the position in this Gospel that Jesus is in complete control. This Gospel has no agony in the garden. Jesus goes to his death not supported by Simon of Cyrene but carrying his own cross. The way of the cross in the Gospel of John is a glorious parade, and Jesus rules from the cross always in control to the smallest detail. "I thirst" has more meaning than Jesus wanting water.

The reaction from the person in the crowd offering bitter wine has always left readers confused. Was someone being nice and offering something to quench the thirst? Why wine, why bitter wine? Was someone being nice to offer Jesus drugged wine to affect the brain and lessen the pain? Was someone being mean to add to the suffering by only adding to the thirst?

Each Gospel records the offering to Jesus of something to drink. In the Gospel of John the author notes that Jesus' saying "I thirst" fulfills the scripture. But what scripture?

Some think Jesus is referring to Psalm 22. This psalm seems to fit Good Friday so well. This psalm has many passages used on Good Friday to show the relationship between the passion and death of Jesus and the Scriptures. "My God, my God, why have you forsaken me?" is taken from this psalm, as already seen.

> But I am a worm and no man, scorned by men
>   and despised by the people.
> All who see me mock at me; they make mouths
>   at me; they wag their heads....
> I am poured out like water, and all my bones are
>   out of joint;

> my heart is like wax; it is melted within my
> breast.
> My strength is dried up like a potsherd, and my
> tongue clings to my mouth....
> They have pierced my hands and my feet;
> they have numbered all my bones.

Jesus is not only aware of the scriptures, but fulfills them as if he knew all along what would happen and what he should do and say. All is part of the plan of God. When he says "I thirst," this does not signify the human condition of Jesus, but he is fulfilling his purpose and destiny in life. He thirsts for completion, for redemption, and for the salvation of humankind. Jesus wants it all to be over and soon it will be. He will have done what God wanted him to do. He thirsts for humanity and for the redemption and salvation of humankind.

In the fourth Gospel the Samaritan woman asked for a drink. Jesus replied, "Whoever drinks of the water that I will give will never thirst. The water that I shall give will become a spring of water welling up to eternal life."

Jesus also says in this Gospel, "If anyone thirsts, let him come to me and drink."

Conclusion

In the Old Testament water is often associated with the Spirit. On Calvary the Mother of Jesus and the Beloved

Disciple receive the Spirit. Their thirst is quenched by the Spirit of Jesus. They symbolize every believer. All who come on Good Friday thirst. They all have been given the gift of the Spirit, and the thirst is quenched.

Prayer for All Creation

> Lord Jesus, because you thirsted for justice and
>   truth,
> The world before me is restored in beauty.
> The world behind me, and below me,
> and above me shines with beauty.
> All things are finished with beauty for all to see;
> Open my eyes to see what you have done.
>
> Amen.

The Sixth Word:
"It is Finished" John 19:30

The last word of Jesus from the cross in the Gospel of John is "It is finished." It does not mean it is over, or finally it is done, this is the end. It means it is completed, it is perfected. It is accomplished. Jesus reigns from the cross in this Gospel, and now he proclaims that he has done what he was destined to do. He is not a failure but a winner. God had given him a mission to accomplish and he has done it. But what exactly has he done?

The prologue of this Gospel, made familiar for anyone over fifty by hearing it read as the last Gospel of every Mass before the reforms of the Second Vatican Council, begins with: "In the beginning was the Word, and the Word was with God, and the Word was God. Through the Word of God all things were created. He came to his own and his own received him not, but to as many as received him he gave them the right to be called children of God. And the Word became flesh and dwelt among us, full of grace and truth."

Jesus came into this world to give people the right to be called children of God. Surely all had been created in the image and likeness of God, but through centuries of sin and failure and neglect on the part of human beings of their God-given dignity they needed to experience redemption. They needed to know that the value and worth and dignity given to them would never be destroyed. They needed to experience the presence of God, and Jesus accomplished all of this.

Anyone who believed in him became part of the family of God. Jesus came to give life and to give it abundantly and this he accomplished; it was completed, perfected, it was finished.

The Word became flesh. Jesus became the human face of God. People of faith could look upon him and experience the presence of God. They could live assured that since he was the resurrection and the life, eternal life not only was promised but had begun. "He who believes in me, even if he dies, will never die." "He who hears my word and believes him who sent me has eternal life. He does not come into judgment but has passed from death to life." "This is eternal life, to know the one true God and Jesus Christ whom he has sent."

People of faith had experienced the presence of God; they had seen the human face of God since they witnessed the compassion, the kindness, the mercy, and the fidelity of Jesus, which mirrored the compassion, kindness, mercy, and fidelity of God.

In the Old Testament certain virtues were always associated with God. The Hebrew words *hesed* and *emeth* describe these virtues. *Emeth* can easily be translated by fidelity or sometimes by truth. Translating *hesed* is more difficult. That is why three English words are often used: compassion, kindness, and mercy or forgiveness.

A compassionate person enters into the experience of another. If the experience is good, it is doubly enjoyed; if painful, the one in need receives help in bearing with the sadness. A kind person always emphasizes what is positive. A mean person will always pick out what is wrong. Mercy means forgiveness.

God demonstrated these qualities in the Old Testament. Now Jesus embodies these same virtues. Jesus entered into the experience of his mother and the couple at the marriage feast of Cana, and the feast continued. The compassionate Jesus responded to the needs of the Samaritan woman and she became an apostle. The kind Jesus could overlook the failings of his disciples. He could see the goodness in the woman taken in adultery, the faith of non-Jews. He always could see the good in others and, as noted, he could forgive those who brought him to Calvary because they did not know what they were doing.

Jesus lived and died faithful to God and faithful to his followers. He did not strike out and curse God for allowing this cruel death. He did not condemn anyone. He had a mission to fulfill and he did it. *It is finished.*

Conclusion

But it is not finished. His followers continue his mission. They offer compassion, kindness, forgiveness, and fidelity. It is finished because Jesus could do no more than he did. Now it is up to those who believe to do likewise.

Prayer of St. Francis
> Lord, make me an instrument of your peace.
> Where there is hatred, let me sow love.
> Where there is injury, pardon.
> Where there is doubt, faith.
> Where there is despair, hope.
> Where there is sadness, joy.
> For it is in giving that we receive,
> In pardoning that we are pardoned,
> And in dying that we are born to eternal life.

The Seventh Word: "Father, into your hands I commend my spirit"
Luke 23:46

And we return to Luke, everyone's favorite Gospel, the Gospel of the kind and gentle Jesus. The Gospel in which Jesus devotes himself to the poor, the oppressed, the marginalized, and especially to women. This Gospel is often called the Gospel of mercy. This is the Gospel of the parable of the lost sheep, the lost coin, and the prodigal son. He alone records the story of the good Samaritan, Martha and Mary, and the widow's mite. And at the end of his life, the gentle Jesus commits himself into the hands of his Father, the hands of a loving God.

This final word from the cross in the Gospel of Luke, Jesus quotes directly from Psalm 31:5. The Psalms have always been the prayer book of Judaism and of Christianity. Surely it also was the prayer book of Jesus since frequently he quotes from the Psalms. After Jesus speaks these words, Luke adds, "and having said this, he breathed his last."

Although this Gospel is filled with gentleness, he also records the pains of Jesus. This evangelist among the Gospels has the agony of Jesus in the garden in which the sweat of Jesus became like great drops of blood (Luke 22:44). After Jesus had successfully resisted the temptations of Satan, the devil departed from Jesus for a while according to Luke 4:13. Now he returns and Jesus enters into battle with him. From the cross Jesus turns evil into good. He forgives those who brought him here. He promises to welcome the good thief into his kingdom. In the death of Jesus the power of evil is conquered. Goodness will prevail through the power of God manifested in the resurrection.

Earlier Luke records the words of Jesus, "I saw Satan fall like lightning from heaven" (Luke 10:18); the victory of Jesus comes only through suffering. The Christian life is lived between "My God, my God, why have you forsaken me?" and "Father, into thy hands I commend my spirit." Would that all we had to do was to live a kind and gentle life and at the end be surrounded by family and friends and say, "Father, into thy hands I commend my spirit." But life is not that way, and even the life of Jesus in the Gospel of Luke was not that way. The most gentle of all the Gospels also records the temptations of Jesus, the failure of disciples, the frustration of Jesus with the rejection by religious leaders, and even the abandonment of his followers, except for some faithful women.

In Mark and Matthew we can identify with Jesus' cry, "My God, my God, why have you abandoned me?" That happens too often in life. Bad things happen to good people. Yet

Jesus knew that God would strengthen him to deal with the pain just as God strengthens us by faith to deal with conflict, suffering, and sorrow. In this final word Luke tells us how to die: thinking of a kind and gentle parent, a father, and giving ourselves into the hands of God.

In the suffering of Jesus and in our own suffering, so much part of human life, we find redemption. Jesus made sure the goodness, the value, and the worth of people would never be destroyed by any power of evil. When we integrate the human pains into our lives, we recognize that the human person is more than just filled with pain. Life is filled with goodness; people are filled with worth, and no amount of sorrow can ever take away that which God has bestowed on every person. And so when we die, we can join Jesus in saying, "Father, into your hands I commend my spirit."

"Father" is the word a child would use in addressing a loving parent. Of course not every one has had a kind and loving father, not everyone has had a kind and loving mother. But if people can think of the best qualities of their father and the best qualities of their mother and add to that the best qualities of those who love you, then God is something like that. We are all related to God as a loving child and should have confidence that this God who gave us life will give us eternal life. The Father of Jesus has his hand on everyone. You can be sure of that.

Conclusion

No one knows how he or she will die; in all probability, most will die alone and with some pain. If during life, we make our own the prayer of Jesus from the cross, "Father, into thy hands I commend my spirit," then when we shall die, that prayer will be in our hearts and on our lips. Then as God the Father welcomed Jesus and proclaimed, "This is my beloved Son in whom I am well pleased," so that same God, the loving parent, will welcome us into paradise and call each of us beloved son or beloved daughter.

Prayer of St. Teresa (author's adaptation)
Let nothing disturb me;
Let nothing frighten me.
All things change;
God alone is changeless.
Patience attains the good.
One who has God lacks nothing.
God alone fills all my needs.

Amen.

IV.
The Sacred Triduum

For centuries the Christian church has set aside the last three days before Easter as a special time of prayer. Just as without the Exodus, Judaism would not have existed, so without the resurrection of the Lord, Christianity would not have existed. The Romans crucified many in the first century of this Common Era and many in Palestine. Without the resurrection Jesus of Nazareth would have remained just another Jew who died at the hands of his fellow Jews and the Roman authorities. With the resurrection human history changed. Now, Jesus as risen Lord could not only give his Spirit to his followers but make possible his presence to his followers in a sacred meal.

The church begins with the commemoration of the sacred meal, the Last Supper, and concludes with a vigil in anticipation of the celebration of the risen Lord in Easter. Throughout these days the church relies on word, ritual, and symbol to bring home to all who participate, the reality of the ministry of Jesus, his suffering and death, but especially his resurrection and his presence to all who call on his name.

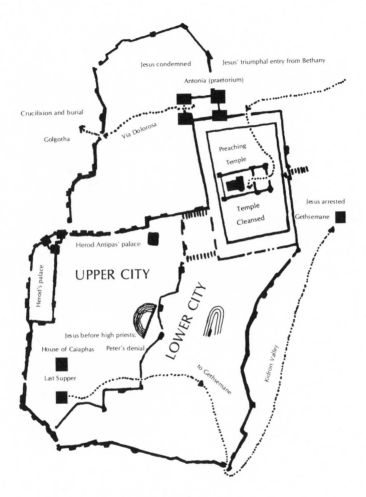

Jerusalem.

Holy Thursday

READ: Exodus 12:1–14 ◆
1 Corinthians 11:23–26 ◆ John 13:1–15

In the Jewish celebration of the Passover seder the youngest member of the family asks: "Why is this night different than all the others?" Christians could ask the same question when they gather to celebrate the Holy Thursday Mass. This is the night it all began. This is the night when Jesus gathered with his disciples to celebrate a farewell meal the night before he died. This is the night when he blessed and broke bread, and blessed and shared a cup of wine with the instruction: "Do this in memory of me."

The ancient Latin hymn says it so well:

O sacrum convivium: O sacred banquet
In quo Christus sumitur: in which Christ is
    consumed,
Recolitur memoria passionis ejus: the memory of
    his passion is recalled,
Mens impletur gratia: the mind is filled with grace,
Pignus datur futurae gloriae: a sign of future glory
    is given.

Such a fitting hymn for Holy Thursday: the past is remembered, the present is acknowledged, and the future is promised, and all is good.

The Jewish Passover recalls how God was good to the Jewish people in the past, and they pray that God will be good to them in the present and in the future. The first reading for Holy Thursday narrates the first Passover experience. Christians on Holy Thursday recall when God was good to them in the past in the life and death of Jesus. They experience the presence of God's grace now, and they look forward to future glory.

In the second reading Paul declares: "We proclaim the death of the Lord until he comes." The past event becomes present, and Christians look for Jesus to come again: past, present, and future.

The Gospel of John has the longest section on the Last Supper yet does not narrate the institution of the Eucharist. Where one might expect to read about the Eucharist, this Gospel narrates that Jesus washes the feet of his disciples. For some this might seem strange. On examining the foot washing, and by comparing it with the crucifixion and then with the Eucharist, something in common becomes evident: Jesus is present to his friends when they are in need; he offers himself and they are changed.

When Jesus washes the feet of his disciples, he performs a menial task usually performed by slaves or servants. He offers himself to them in this action and they become better: they share in his inheritance and then they should minister to each other.

On Calvary Jesus joins the fate of all humans. He accepts death since all must die. He offers himself to God with confidence, and human history is changed. Redemption and salvation have taken place for all. The value, the worth, and the dignity of every human being Jesus preserves. He has redeemed people. And even in a cruel death, God is present to all who trust in God.

In the Eucharist Jesus is present to his friends, offers himself as food and drink, and those who receive him are joined to God through the gift of Jesus. In the Eucharist the followers of Jesus receive a pledge of God's continuing presence in their lives and wish each other peace. They become better people.

Jesus warned his followers, "In the world you will have trouble, but have a light heart; I have overcome the world" (John 16:33). In the celebration of Holy Thursday, Christians recall how God was good to them in the past, will be good to them NOW, and in the future, for God has given them Jesus. "If God has given us his Son, is there anything God will deny us?" (Rom 8:32).

Conclusion

Holy Thursday gives hope for the future. Christians know Jesus remains with them in the Eucharist. People are already redeemed. Their value, worth, and dignity can never be destroyed for Jesus has said so. People have experienced the positive presence of God in the past and in the present and will continue to experience the saving presence of God in the future. Christians can remain of good cheer, with a light heart, for the Lord Jesus has overcome the world.

Prayer for Holy Thursday

O sacred banquet in which Christ is received,
the memory of his passion is recalled,
the soul is filled with grace, and we receive a
    pledge of future glory,
let me never forget what I have received.

Amen.

Good Friday

READ: Isaiah 52:13—53:12 ◆
John 18:1—19:42

Usually when people think of Good Friday, they think of pain and sorrow and the agony and death of Jesus. For more than twelve hundred years, however, the church has read the passion according to John on Good Friday, and in this Gospel Jesus experiences no pain nor suffering. The way of the cross is a triumphant parade.

The Gospel of John has no agony in the garden and no pain. Jesus acts in control at all times and even tells his captors what they must do. When he proclaims that "I am" (a substitute for the name of God in Hebrew), they all fall down in an appropriate gesture in the presence of the divine. Jesus needs no one to help him carry the cross. On the cross Jesus reigns with a concern for his mother, and his mother together with the Beloved Disciple, the two perfect disciples, receive his Spirit. He proclaims "it is finished." Jesus has accomplished redemption for the human race.

Throughout this Gospel, Jesus reveals God as compassionate, merciful, kind, and faithful. Jesus has lived and will die as the human face of God. Redemption is accomplished.

The value, worth, and dignity given to every human being by being created in the image and likeness of God will never be destroyed. Even if individuals try to destroy this gift of God, Jesus has seen to it that this value will never be lost or destroyed.

In Jesus people have experienced the saving presence of God. God has entered into human history in the life and ministry of Jesus, and now as he dies, he manifests how God can be present in every human dying even in a cruel death.

Good Friday celebrates the triumph of goodness over evil. When people try to destroy what is good, God intervenes and will not allow it. The human family tried to say no to goodness by bringing Jesus to Calvary, but God has said yes to the power of goodness in Jesus, and so Jesus reigns in death, which issues in the resurrection.

In the midst of a sad and often painful world, Jesus gives to his followers always a reason to rejoice. People experience the presence of God in the thousand ways life is made more pleasant. Moments of salvation take place when winter gives way to spring as the world takes on a newness that lightens the step of everyone. When people send a thank-you note or flowers or make a telephone call or visit the sick, each becomes a moment when God becomes present in life through the kindness of others.

Good Friday accomplished redemption and salvation, and thus in the Gospel of John pain and suffering give way to the joy and happiness of God's saving presence. Jesus has thirsted for people to experience God's presence. Jesus has fulfilled a ministry in which people have seen and observed and experienced forgiveness, compassion, kindness, and fidelity. Calvary has made salvation and redemption possible. Now people not only must acknowledge how they have experienced the goodness of God, but must in turn offer to others what they have experienced.

Conclusion

Good Friday should not be a day of mourning. People should have done that on Palm Sunday. Since the Gospel of John is read at the Good Friday service, Good Friday should be a day of rejoicing in what God has done for the human race through Jesus, including his death. Since Jesus has made salvation possible for all people, especially followers of him should contribute to moments of salvation in each other's lives. The glorious parade to Calvary in the Gospel of John has led to the life-giving death of Jesus, and then he gave the Spirit to his perfect disciples, his mother and the Beloved Disciple. *Rejoice. Good Friday is here!*

Prayer to the Mother of the Lord to Intercede

> Holy Mother of our Savior, intercede for us.
> Help us to accept the redemption offered to us.
> Guide us into following the inspiration of the
>   Holy Spirit.
> Let the word of your Son be made flesh anew in
>   our lives.
> As we follow the way of the cross,
> may we always see the presence of God
> in every moment of life,
> even in dying.
> And through your intercession, may we give to
>   each other moments of
> salvation.
>
> Amen.

Holy Saturday

READ: Genesis 1:1—2:2 ◆ Genesis 22:1–18
Exodus 14:15—15:1 ◆ Isaiah 55:1–11
Ezekiel 36:16–28 ◆ Romans 6:3–11
Matthew 28:1–10 or Mark 16:1–8 or
Luke 24:1–12

The holiest night of the Christian year offers a super-abundance of images and symbols. Darkness gives way to light. Fire and water, primal elements, interact with promises of life. Solemnity and somberness turn into happiness and joy. Music and bells shatter the silence. The long days of Lent usher in the joyful exuberance of Easter.

The long vigil of readings narrates the history of God's dealings with people. God first set things in order. "In the beginning God created (set in order) the heavens and the earth. And the earth was a formless waste *(tohu we bohu)*. And the Spirit of God hovered over the waters." Into the chaos of the earth came the Spirit of God to battle disorder *(tohu we bohu)* and win! Now things are as they should be. And to humans God gave the command to continue to struggle over disorder and win.

God asked Abraham to give up his past, family, and land and to trust in God, for God told him to move to a new land. God asked Abraham to give up his future in the sacrifice of Isaac. And Abraham trusted in God, and God justified Abraham. Abraham could stand in God's presence because of his faith.

God called Moses to lead his people to safety and freedom, and Moses responded. The people of Israel became the people of God, and God showed them that God would be present to them in good days and in bad.

Isaiah could sit on a pile of rubble and say: "This too shall rise!" The desert will blossom and the lion will lie down with the lamb. Hope springs eternal even in the midst of destruction and sorrow.

Ezekiel the priest who lost everything—position, power, wealth, and family—believed in a future when God will give a new spirit and a new heart. Things will improve. God has been good to the people in the past, and God will be good to the people of God again.

Paul celebrates the gift of baptism in water. People are given new life. Their faith has enriched them and made it possible to live according to the spirit and teachings of Jesus.

Finally Jesus, the risen Lord, is present to his friends whenever they are in need. No one should ever feel alone or forgotten or not loved and appreciated. The risen Lord accompanies all of his followers in their lives and will be present also when they die. He promises a similar resurrection to new and eternal life.

Conclusion

The Spirit of God continues the work of overcoming chaos and disorder. Baptism begins the life of the Spirit. The crucified and risen Lord offers the Spirit to all who believe. Baptism begins the process of allowing the Spirit of God to fill in the nooks and crannies of the dying human personality as soon as the believer has invited the Spirit of God to fill in all that is lacking. The chaos of every human life gives way to the perfection and fulfillment of the promise given when God created male and female in the image and likeness of God.

The chaos of winter and Lent has passed. The spring of life and order has dawned. Easter promises eternal life when everything is as it should be. Order takes over the human mind and heart and body, and the Spirit continues the work of salvation and redemption. Jesus is risen, Alleluia, alleluia!

Prayer of Thanksgiving

Lord God, I thank you for the gift of Jesus your
Son.
Creator and Father,
I celebrate my belief in Jesus as my Redeemer
and Savior.
God, Father and Son,
I thank you for the gift of your Spirit to help me
set all things in order.
Creator, Redeemer, and Sanctifier,
you have blessed me with the gift of baptism.
May I also be grateful for life and faith
and look for the fulfillment of my hopes in
eternal life.
May the resurrected Lord continue to fill me
with the Spirit
that enables me to call you my God and my
Father forever.

Amen.

Easter Sunday

READ: Acts 10:34–43
Colossians 3:1–4 ◆ John 20:1–28

Easter, like spring, celebrates life, rebirth, hope, and joy. Jesus lives. Jesus is risen, living among his friends. Jesus did not suffer the fate of all humanity by dying to remain the dead master and teacher. Jesus has been raised from the dead. This faith, Christians celebrate every spring.

The resurrection of Jesus makes Jesus different from all other persons. His resurrection makes believers different as well. No longer must people remain suspended between hope and despair, darkness and light. One like us in all things but sin has been the faithful and loving Son of God, and so God has blessed the human race and all creation, and God has given hope to all.

The readings from the Acts of the Apostles offer a good summary of Christian preaching. Jesus was filled with the Spirit of God. He went around doing good. He died and was raised and will come again. Peter preaches and people respond by believing, by changing their way of living and being baptized into the community of faith, the church.

Throughout These Forty Days We Pray

The church has always preached the same good news. His followers are Easter people. The resurrection drives out all gloom and fills life with joy and expectation, which will bind the days into years and the years into a lifetime.

Paul can sing a hymn of joy, for Christ lives and his followers share in the joy that binds Jesus to all believers. Those who follow the Lord are never condemned to the past but move with determination into the future, which is a good future. As God raised Jesus, so believers can look forward to their good future for their future is God.

All of the resurrection stories involve Jesus responding to his friends when they were in need. Peter and the Beloved Disciple run to the tomb, confused after hearing the testimony of Mary. They both look in. The Beloved Disciple believes.

In some ways the fourth Gospel displays little interest in the resurrection of Jesus. For this author, the death of Jesus is the hour of his exaltation and glorification. When Jesus died he handed over his Spirit (19:30), and the two perfect disciples, the Mother of Jesus and the Beloved Disciple, were present to receive it. Death, resurrection, ascension, and Pentecost coalesce on Calvary in this Gospel.

When the author treats the resurrection appearances, he has a distinct purpose. In each case the disciples are troubled and confused. God glorifies Jesus in his death, and in his resurrection Jesus returns to give birth to faith and to encourage and aid his followers. Now that Jesus is risen, people can understand that by living and dying as all people must die, Jesus made it possible for all to live a good human

A garden tomb.

life and die a good human death supported and comforted by the presence of God.

In this final Gospel, Jesus responded to the needs of his followers. Mary was disconsolate and felt alone. Jesus called her by name and her problems vanished. The disciples were gathered in fear and Jesus wished them only peace. Thomas had his doubts and the presence of Jesus made him proclaim, "My Lord and my God." The disciples labored and caught nothing in their nets. Jesus came and they caught 153 fish. In each instance the presence of Jesus responded to their needs and the outcome was favorable.

Conclusion

On Easter Christians gather as a community to profess faith and become more aware of how much this faith needs to grow. On Easter Christians turn to the risen Lord to ask for a deepening of faith, aware that Jesus is always present to his friends, especially when they need him. Jesus lives today among his followers as he was present to his earliest followers.

On Easter Christians listen to the word of God and celebrate the presence of the risen Lord in the Eucharist. In a troubled world and a troubled church in the midst of a personal life mixed with joy and sorrow, the presence of Jesus heals and consoles. Jesus lives. Happy Easter.

Easter Prayer
> Risen Lord and Redeemer, you have given me
>   hope in life.
> Your presence brings comfort.
> When I am down, you lift me up;
> When I am glad, you double the joy.
> Strengthen my faith and trust in you.
> Support my hope with your promise of life.
> Increase my love for you, for others, and for all
>   of creation.
> I make my prayer to you, filled with your Spirit
> and trusting in God, your Father and mine.
>   Amen.

Appendix:
Parish Lenten Holy Hour

Sample

<small>OUTLINE OF EVENING PROGRAM FOR FIRST WEEK OF LENT:</small>
REPENTANCE

1. **Opening Lenten Hymn:** "Lord, throughout These Forty Days of Lent We Pray"
2. **Opening Prayer:**
   Good and gracious God,
   > you have a great and loving plan for our world
   >   and for us.
   Through our observance of Lent
   > we hope to share in that plan faithfully and joyfully.
   Help us to understand your will,
   > to be attentive to the signs that you give us
   > as we fast, pray, and respond to the needs of others
   >   by works of charity.
   We make our prayer through Christ our Lord. Amen.
3. **Reading from Scripture:** Psalm 51
4. **Homily**
5. **Silent Meditation**

6. **Musical Motet:** *"Attende domine et miserere, quia peccavimus tibi"*

7. **Closing Prayer:**

> Hear us, O Lord, and have mercy, for we have sinned.
>
> Pardon us, O Lord Jesus, those whom your passion and death have redeemed.
>
> Keep us from evil and sin, and fill us with your Holy Spirit
>
> as we turn to you and change our way of living. Amen.

8. **Blessing:**

> Through the passion, death, and resurrection of Jesus,
>
> > God has redeemed you and made you children of God.
>
> May God bless you with joy.
>
> The Redeemer has given you lasting freedom.
> May he reward you with everlasting life.
>
> Through your Lenten observance,
> > may the Holy Spirit fill you with hope
> > and guide you in faith and love.
>
> These blessings may our good and gracious God always bestow upon you,
> > God who is Father, Son, and Holy Spirit.
> > > Amen.